CUBA

Anna Cavallo

Lerner Publications Company • Minneapolis

Lerner Publications Company
A division of Lerner Publishing Group, Inc.
241 First Avenue North
Minneapolis, MN 55401 U.S.A.

Website address: www.lernerbooks.com

Library of Congress Cataloging-in-Publication Data

Cavallo, Anna.
    Cuba / by Anna Cavallo.
        p.   cm. — (Country explorers)
    Includes index.
    ISBN 978–0–7613–5317–1 (lib. bdg. : alk. paper)
    1. Cuba—Juvenile literature. I. Title.
    F1758.5.C38 2011
    972.91—dc22   2009042322

Manufactured in the United States of America
1 – VI – 7/15/10

Table of Contents

Welcome!	4		In Good Health	30
The Land	6		Families	32
A Sea of Life	8		Homes	34
Two Seasons	10		Religion	36
Early Cubans	12		Music and Dance	38
People	14		Vacation Spot	40
New Leaders	16		Sports and Games	42
Havana	18		*The Flag of Cuba*	*44*
Holidays	20		*Fast Facts*	*45*
Made in Cuba	22		*Glossary*	*46*
Getting Around	24		*To Learn More*	*47*
Food	26		*Index*	*48*
School	28			

Welcome!

We're heading to Cuba! Cuba is an island country. It reaches from the Gulf of Mexico on its west coast to the Atlantic Ocean on its east coast. The Caribbean Sea touches Cuba's southern coast.

The Bahamas and the U.S. state of Florida are Cuba's neighbors to the north. Jamaica lies to the south. Haiti is Cuba's closest neighbor. It sits to the southeast.

Varadero Beach is one of Cuba's many beautiful, sandy beaches.

4

The Land

Low plains and rolling hills make up much of Cuba. Farmland and tropical trees cover these areas.

Mountains rise beyond green farm fields and tropical trees.

Mountains rise up in other parts of the country. The Sierra Maestra is a mountain range in the southeast. It includes Pico Turquino, the island's highest point. The Organos and the Rosario ranges lie in western Cuba.

Map Whiz Quiz

Take a look at the map on page 5. Trace the outline of Cuba onto a sheet of paper. Can you find the tip of Florida? Mark that with an N for north. What about Haiti? Label it with an E for east. Find Jamaica. Mark it with an S for south. Then color the water around Cuba blue.

A gentle mist hovers over the treetops along the Sierra Maestra mountain range.

A Sea of Life

Coral reefs form just off Cuba's coasts. Reefs are ridges.
Tiny animals called coral polyps build them.

This tropical
fish is called a
sergeant major.
It is swimming over
fan corals off
Cuba's coast.

8

Coral reefs are full of life. Small fish, eels, sponges, and other sea animals make their homes in the reefs. This gives them protection. Turtles, sharks, and other large fish roam in the area, hunting for food.

Different types of coral grow at the bottom of the Caribbean Sea.

Two Seasons

Cuba is warm all year. The island has just two seasons. The dry season runs from November to April. May through October is the rainy season.

Guests at these tourist hotels can relax by the shore or play in the surf of the Caribbean Sea.

Hurricanes can strike during the rainy season. These storms form over ocean water. They bring lots of rain and strong winds. Hurricanes often cause flooding along the coasts.

Guantánamo Bay

The U.S. Navy has kept a base at Guantánamo Bay, Cuba, since 1903. The base is on the southern coast. It is the oldest U.S. military base outside the United States.

After a hurricane, a tree blocks a sidewalk in Havana, the capital of Cuba.

Early Cubans

Some of the first people to live in Cuba were Arawak Indians. One group lived in villages. They farmed, hunted, and fished. They also made statues and canoes.

An Arawak village in the 1400s would have looked like this. This village is part of a museum in eastern Cuba.

But in 1492, Spanish explorers sailed to Cuba. They claimed the island for Spain. Soon the Spanish took over. Spain ruled Cuba for four hundred years. Cuba became a separate country in 1902.

Cuban Slaves

The Spanish settlers made the Arawak people work as slaves. Most Arawaks died from sickness or bad treatment. Then the Spanish brought slaves from Africa to work for them. Cuban slavery ended in 1886.

In this engraving from 1683, slaves are working for the Spanish owners of a sugar plantation (a large farm).

People

Many people in modern Cuba have ancestors (long-ago relatives) who were Spanish settlers. Other Cubans have African roots.

These Cuban musicians are of African descent. They are playing drums for a crowd in Havana.

14

About half of Cubans are a mixture of Spanish, African, and Arawak backgrounds. They make up the largest group. A small number of Chinese people live in Cuba too.

Some Cuban schoolchildren have ancestors from many different ethnic groups.

New Leaders

Cubans fought against Spanish rulers again and again. Finally, in the 1950s, a soldier named Fulgencio Batista took power. But he did little to help most Cubans.

Fulgencio Batista (*center*) meets with reporters in 1954.

Fidel Castro forced him out of power in 1959. Castro became the new leader. He is Cuba's most famous leader. Castro ruled for nearly fifty years. Then his brother Raul Castro became the ruler.

Cuban Communism

Castro formed a Communist government. This kind of government owns most businesses and homes. Communist governments limit people's freedoms and ways to make money.

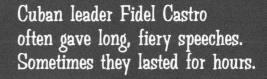

Cuban leader Fidel Castro often gave long, fiery speeches. Sometimes they lasted for hours.

Havana

Havana sits on Cuba's north coast. The capital is home to government offices and universities. More than two million people live in the city.

People flock to colorful Calle Obispo, a busy shopping street in Havana.

18

In Old Havana, historic buildings line the streets. Musicians and dancers entertain people in open squares. People can buy roasted nuts and other snacks at food stands.

Dear Mom and Dad,

Today we are visiting Havana! We learned that many ships use Havana's port. We saw old buildings and city squares called plazas. We also went for a stroll on El Malecón. It is a walkway next to the ocean. We even got fresh pineapple juice!

See you soon!
Jenny

Havana, Cuba

Holidays

Several holidays honor important days in Cuba's history. On January 1, Cubans celebrate Liberation Day. That is the day Fidel Castro won power in 1959. Cubans gather in city squares to hear leaders speak. People relax and enjoy music and dancing.

Cubans wave flags during a parade to celebrate Liberation Day.

National Revolution Day begins on July 25. It is a three-day holiday. The holiday marks a battle that Fidel Castro led in 1953. In December, many people celebrate Christmas.

Crowds gather to watch fireworks during Christmas week.

Made in Cuba

For a long time, Cuba produced more sugar than any other country. Sugarcane is still the most common crop. Farmers also grow oranges, coffee, and rice. Nickel, a metal, is mined in the ground in southeastern Cuba.

Sugarcane is an important crop in Cuba. Here, the sugarcane is being cut and gathered for processing.

Fishing is also a big business in Cuba. Fishing boats sail in the Caribbean Sea and the Atlantic Ocean. They catch lobster, shrimp, snails, tuna, and other fish. Cuba sells much of this catch to other countries.

Fishers bring in their daily catch.

Getting Around

Cuba's streets are filled with people on foot and on bicycles. Cars, motorcycles, taxis, and buses also get people where they need to go. And tourists can ride around Havana in *cocotaxis*. These small, open taxis are shaped like eggs!

Bicitaxis are another way for tourists to ride around Havana. These small, open taxis are pulled by bicycles.

24

Many people get around Cuba on foot.

Cuban Cars

Many cars in Cuba look like U.S. classic cars *(below)*. That's because they are. Car companies in the United States sent them to Cuba in the 1940s and the 1950s. After Castro took power, U.S. companies stopped selling cars to Cuba. Cubans have been driving and repairing these old cars since then.

Food

Cubans often eat rice and beans at dinner. Meals might also include pork, chicken, or fish. Slices of tomatoes and cucumbers add color to the meal.

Chicken in black bean and tomato sauce, served with brown rice, make a traditional Cuban stew.

Fried plantains *(front)* make up part of a tasty breakfast meal.

Food for Free— Almost

Many Cubans have little money for food. So each month, the government provides some foods at very low cost. Cubans usually get rice, beans, bread rolls, and potatoes. Meat, sugar, and salt are included too. Families with children also get eggs and milk.

Do you ever eat fried fruit? Plantains are a kind of banana. Cubans fry them for a tasty treat. People enjoy fresh oranges, pineapples, mangoes, and papayas too. Sweet pastries are also popular treats.

School

All kids in Cuba start school at the age of five. They stay in school until the age of fifteen. They study math, science, government, history, and Spanish. Then they may go to high school. That prepares them for college or for a job-training school. All education is free, including college.

A teacher stops to help a student at this Havana elementary school.

28

What do you wear to school? Cuban students wear uniforms. Students in grades one through six wear red scarves around their necks.

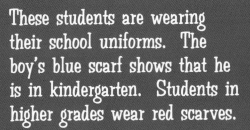

These students are wearing their school uniforms. The boy's blue scarf shows that he is in kindergarten. Students in higher grades wear red scarves.

In Good Health

Cuba is known for its good health care. Anyone can see a doctor or go to a hospital for free. But medicine can be hard to get.

This baby is being cared for in one of Havana's excellent hospitals.

Doctors work to keep people healthy. This helps most Cubans to live long lives.

A group of elderly friends get together in Havana.

Families

Cuban families are close. They often live together in small houses or apartments. Parents, children, and grandparents may live together. Kids usually live at home until they get married.

This grandmother relaxes with her family in their living room.

La Familia

Here are some of the Spanish words for family members.

father	padre	(PAH-dray)
mother	madre	(MAH-dray)
brother	hermano	(air-MAH-no)
sister	hermana	(air-MAH-nah)
uncle	tío	(TEE-oh)
aunt	tía	(TEE-ah)
grandpa	abuelo	(ah-BWAY-loh)
grandma	abuela	(ah-BWAY-lah)

A large Cuban family poses with their car. They are vacationing at a seaside resort.

Homes

Most Cubans live in cities. Concrete apartment buildings fill city blocks. Apartments are usually crowded. Many buildings are not in good shape. They have peeling paint and chipped or cracked walls.

Laundry hangs from some of the balconies of this apartment building in Havana. The building dates back to when Spain ruled Cuba.

34

Cubans living in small towns or in the country often have houses made of clay, mud bricks, or concrete. In many places, there are not enough homes. Lots of people live in each crowded house. The government builds homes for people in some of these areas.

A family of coconut workers poses on the front porch of their country home.

Religion

Many Cubans are Roman Catholics. Protestant and Evangelical Christians make up a much smaller group. Others are Jewish or belong to no religion.

People gather in the square in front of Havana Cathedral. The Catholic church was built in the 1700s.

Santeria is a major religion in Cuba. It combines Catholicism with spirit worship. Slaves from Africa worshipped spirits called *orishas*. But Spanish slave owners wanted their slaves to become Catholic. So slaves used Catholic saints as their orishas. The slaves tricked their owners into thinking they were worshipping the saints.

These women make offerings *(on the ground)* at a Santeria ceremony in Havana.

Music and Dance

Music and dance are at the heart of Cuban culture. Cuban music combines Spanish guitars with African drumbeats. Maracas and claves add lively rhythm. Claves are wooden sticks. *Son* music pairs the two instruments with songs about love or the country.

This band performs on stage in Havana. Notice the front musician holding a clave and maraca.

Mambo, rumba, and salsa came from son music. Each of these is a dance as well as a musical style. Men twirl women and lead them around the dance floor. Colorful skirts swish and spin as the women dance.

The Cuban band Los 4 Vientos (The Four Winds) performs with dancers on the streets of Havana.

Vacation Spot

Cuba has become a popular vacation spot for people from Canada and Europe. Winter travelers enjoy its warm weather. And the money travelers spend helps Cuba's economy.

Tourists sunbathe on a beach in Varadero.

Restaurants and hotels get a lot of business from tourists. Also, Cubans can earn money working at jobs that help travelers.

Cuban Money

Cuba uses two different kinds of money. Cubans use both pesos and convertible pesos. Workers are paid in both. They can buy things such as groceries with pesos. But places that serve lots of tourists use convertible pesos. One convertible peso is about equal to one U.S. dollar. One peso is worth much less.

Vacationers take photos with an old man and his donkey. They are in the city of Trinidad on Cuba's southern coast.

Sports and Games

Cubans love to play and watch baseball. It is the island's national sport. Soccer, boxing, basketball, and track and field are also popular.

These young men enjoy a game of baseball in Santa Clara, in central Cuba.

42

The game of dominoes is another favorite Cuban pastime. Players match up dotted tiles end to end. Friends play while talking and catching up. People also gather in parks or squares to play.

These players sit outside their Havana house for a game of dominoes.

THE FLAG OF CUBA

Cuba's flag has three blue stripes that run from left to right. They form the top, bottom, and middle stripes of the flag. They are separated by two white stripes. A red triangle juts from the left side of the flag. A white star is in the center of the triangle. The blue stripes stand for the three parts into which Cuba was divided long ago. The white stripes are for independence. The red triangle stands for the blood of those who died fighting for independence. And the white star stands for freedom. This became the Cuban national flag on May 20, 1902.

FAST FACTS

FULL COUNTRY NAME: Republic of Cuba

AREA: 42,803 square miles (110,860 square kilometers), or slightly smaller than the state of Pennsylvania

MAIN LANDFORMS: the mountain ranges Sierra Maestra, Organos, and Rosario; rock formations at Valle de Viñales; the Zapata and Lanier swamps; rolling plains; Isla de la Juventud

MAJOR RIVER: Cauto

ANIMALS AND THEIR HABITATS: coral polyps, dolphins, jellyfish, manatees, rays, sharks, swordfish (ocean water off coasts); deer (plains and throughout); hutias, solenodons, wild boars; boas, geckos, snails, tree frogs (throughout); Cuban crocodiles (Zapata and Lanier swamps, Isla de la Juventud); flamingos (northern coast)

CAPITAL CITY: Havana

OFFICIAL LANGUAGE: Spanish

POPULATION: about 11,451,650

GLOSSARY

ancestor: a relative who lived long ago

Arawaks: native peoples who lived in Cuba and other parts of the Caribbean and South America before the Spanish arrived

classic: a good example of something; something old but in good condition

cocotaxis: open, round taxis that have two passenger seats and three wheels

Communism: a system of government in which the government owns all or most businesses and property

coral reef: a rocky reef built from the hard skeletons of coral polyps

economy: the system of earning and spending money in a country

historic: from a long time ago

hurricane: a violent storm with strong, swirling winds. Hurricanes start over the ocean near the equator and can travel great distances before hitting coastal land.

plantains: large, greenish fruits similar to bananas

port: a place where ships and boats can dock to load or unload supplies

revolution: the forcing out of one government, often with violence, to replace it with another

TO LEARN MORE

BOOKS

Braithwaite, Jill. *From Cane to Sugar.* Minneapolis: Lerner Publications Company, 2004. Learn the step-by-step process used to make sugar from sugarcane.

Chambers, Veronica. *Celia Cruz, Queen of Salsa.* New York: Dial Books for Young Readers, 2005. Read about Celia Cruz, the Cuban singer who helped make salsa music popular around the world.

Doeden, Matt. *Hurricanes.* Minneapolis: Lerner Publishing Company, 2008. Find out how hurricanes form, what they do, and how they are tracked.

Marx, Trish. *Reaching for the Sun.* Minneapolis: Millbrook Press, 2003. Learn what life is like for Cuban kids by following American students as they visit Cuba for a theater project.

WEBSITES

Cuba
http://kids.nationalgeographic.com/
Places/Find/Cuba
Visit this National Geographic Kids website to check out facts and photos, watch a video about Cuba, or send an e-card.

Cuban Flag Quiz/Printout
http://www.enchantedlearning.com/
northamerica/cuba/flag/flagquizbw.shtml
Learn more about Cuba's flag, take a short quiz, and fill in the flag's colors.

INDEX

families, 32–33
food, 19, 26–27

games, 43

holidays, 20–21
houses, 32, 34–35

map of Cuba, 4–5
music, 14, 19, 20, 38–39

people, 12–15
politics, 16–17

religion, 36–37

schools, 28–29
sports, 42

transportation, 24–25

The images in this book are used with the permission of: © age fotostock/SuperStock, p. 4; © Peter Treanor/Art Directors & TRIP, p. 6; © Angelo Cavalli/SuperStock, pp. 7, 38; © Andrew Rubtsov/Alamy, p. 8; © Vivatum/Dreamstime.com, p. 9; © Rubens Abboud/Alamy, p. 10; © Barry Lewis/Alamy, pp. 11, 42; © Ian Nellist/Alamy, p. 12; The Art Archive/Biblioteca Nacional Madrid/Gianni Dagli Orti , p. 13; © Julio Etchart/Alamy, p. 14; © Gus Bradley/Alamy, pp. 15, 19; © Bettmann/CORBIS, p. 16; © Stephen Ferry/Getty Images, p. 17; © Alex Segre/Alamy, p. 18; © Alejandro Ernesto/ZUMA Press, p. 20; © Lonely Planet/SuperStock, p. 21; © Geoffrey Roughton/Alamy, p. 22; © Amos Nachoum/CORBIS, p. 23; © STR/epa/CORBIS, p. 24; © Alex Segre/Alamy, p. 25 (top/left); © Franxyz/Dreamstime.com, p. 25 (bottom/right); © Paulcowan/Dreamstime.com, p. 26; © Monkey Business Images/Dreamstime.com, p. 27; © Robert Wallis/Panos Pictures, p. 28; © 1bestofphoto/Alamy, p. 29; © Robert Wallis/Panos Pictures, p. 30; © David White/Alamy, p. 31; © allover Photography/Alamy, p. 32; © Susanna Bennett/Alamy, p. 33; © Christine Osborne Pictures/Alamy, p. 34; © James Quine/Alamy, p. 35; © Kmiragaya/Dreamstime.com, p. 36; © Mireille Vautier/Alamy, p. 37; © Sami Sarkia Travel America/Alamy, p. 39; © Rolf Richardson/Alamy, p. 40; © Bill Bachmann/Alamy, p. 41; © amjadel-geoushi/Alamy, p. 43, © Laura Westlund/Independent Picture Service, p. 44; Illustrations by © Bill Hauser/Independent Picture Service.

Cover: © Art Wolfe/Getty Images.